You & God

Adapted From Material Written By

**Roberta Bonnici • Craig Froman
Richard L. Schoonover • Gary Speer
Louis T. Smith • John A. Thomas
Larry Thomas**

Radiant Life

1445 Boonville Avenue
Springfield, Missouri 65802–1894
02-0150

National Director: Arlyn R. Pember
Editor in Chief: Michael H. Clarensau
Adult Editor: Paul W. Smith
Series Coordinator: Aaron D. Morgan
Design/Cover Illustration: Jared Van Bruaene

Printed in the United States of America

ISBN 0–88243–150–1

The leader guide for this book can be ordered from Gospel Publishing
House (02–0250) at 1–800–641–4310.

Contents

Preface

You & God, one of four books in the *Biblical Living Series*, will help you explore what the Bible has to say about your relationship with the Lord—how to develop it, how it can benefit you, and how it can change the way you think and act. Each chapter will help you evaluate relevant Bible passages by asking you thought-provoking questions, many of which call on you to make application to your personal life.

You can read *You & God* on its own or as part of the *Biblical Living Series*. It is recommended you read only one chapter a week so you can allow each chapter's biblical truths and instructions time to "sink in." Some of the questions will require ongoing action on your part; do not neglect these if you want to get the full benefit from this book.

If you are reading *You & God* as part of a small group or Sunday School class, be sure to read and complete the assigned chapter before each meeting. The discussions, work sheets, and activities in which you will participate during your group's next meeting will be most beneficial if you have read and filled out the chapter being covered.

   This preface would not be complete without recognizing the authors whose studies for Radiant Life's young adult and adult dated curriculum were adapted for this book. Roberta Bonnici is an associate pastor and freelance writer. Craig Froman is the registrar of Berean University. Richard L. Schoonover is the technical editor of *Enrichment Journal.* Gary Speer is a freelance writer. Louis T. Smith and John A. Thomas pastor churches. Larry Thomas is both a pastor and the Sunday School Training Coordinator for the Assemblies of God.

                                   Aaron Morgan
                                   Biblical Living Series Coordinator
                                   Springfield, Missouri

Part One

Communicating With God

How well do you know God? Regardless of how close a relationship you have with the Lord, you can always learn more about and from Him.

In the next three chapters, you will be challenged to meet every day with the Lord, taking the time necessary to build an intimate relationship with Him. You will be taught the importance of individual worship and prayer as proper and effective ways of communicating with God. Throughout, you will be reminded that this communication is always to be two way.

Chapter 3 looks at the Lord's Prayer as recorded in the Book of Luke and the teachings about prayer that follow. You will learn to look beyond these familiar words to the principles of effective praying behind them.

More important than "getting through" these chapters is applying them to your daily life. Make it your goal to increase the time you spend each day communicating with God.

Spending Time With God

Busy, busy, busy! Does that describe you? If so, you are not alone. The majority of today's adults juggle social and family obligations with hectic work schedules. Each activity you participate in demands a certain amount of time. If you are like most people, you do not have enough time in the day to do everything that needs to be done. Yet, as a Christian, another responsibility calls for its own portion of your time—daily devotions.

One way to manage a busy schedule is to take a close look at the purpose behind each task. You can determine which tasks are most important by evaluating how important their outcomes are. This method of prioritizing can help you decide what activities can wait and what things have to be done promptly or consistently.

So to understand why you need to make daily devotions a priority on your schedule, you need to understand why these times are so valuable. This chapter will focus on the purpose and benefits of personal devotions. Hopefully this will lead you to maintain your personal devotional life as an "every day" event (Psalm 145:2).

Knowing God And Yourself

Think of a conversation between close friends, two people who truly want to spend time with each other. More than words are spoken. Body language is read, feelings are expressed, and the relationship is strengthened. As the two people converse, each has the opportunity to get to know the other better.

A similar thing happens when you participate in daily devotions. Communing with God through prayer, the Word, and worship provides you with a time to learn about God. He is also given opportunity to probe your heart and minister to your needs. Your relationship with Him is strengthened.

This truth is demonstrated throughout the Psalms. In Psalm 42:1,2 the writer compared himself to a deer that "pants for streams of water." The Psalmist expressed his deep yearning for God. More than a mere sense of obligation drove the Psalmist to seek God; it was need.

This motive is apparent in Psalm 63:1. In this passage, David used strong words to describe his desire for God. A sense of need is the fuel that gives daily devotions vibrancy and life. You come to God daily, not simply because you are obligated, but because you want to learn more about Him.

1–1. *Have you been thinking of daily devotions as a need or a chore? How has that attitude affected the time you have spent with God lately?*

Where does time with God lead? For David, it led not only to a deeper knowledge of God, but also of himself.

Read Psalm 139:23,24. David asked God to examine him thoroughly, exposing any wickedness that would cause him to stray from the way of everlasting life. In other words, through his time with God, David would allow God to correct any problems he had in his life. The more time David spent with the Lord, the more insight he would have into his character as God revealed things to him about himself.

Paul expressed the same feelings in Philippians 3:10,11. Like the Psalmist, he yearned for a deeper knowledge of God. "I want to know Christ," he said in verse 10. What was the result of that desire? It was much more than simply knowing more facts about Jesus. Paul wanted to know Christ because he wanted to be like Him (verse 10). He knew that he would better himself as his relationship with God grew stronger.

It is the same for you. You can grow in your knowledge of the Lord, and even come to know yourself better, when you spend time with God. Like close friends emerging from a time of fellowship with one another, you can leave your time with the Lord stimulated and strengthened.

1–2.   *What is something you have learned about yourself from times you have spent with God?*

Communicating With God

Along with providing you with the opportunity to know God and yourself, daily devotions also give you a time to communicate with God. This idea pervades the Psalms. Many of those who wrote the Psalms called on God for help in times of need. The word *cry* appears more than 40 times in the Psalms, often as a plea for God to help His people.

Look at three examples from the Psalms. First, David pleaded with the Lord to listen to his cry in Psalm 5:1,2. Verse 2 shows you that David knew the Lord was his only source of help. He called out to his King and his God.

David again mentioned his "sighing" in Psalm 38:9. In Psalm 5, the sighing was brought on by the threat of David's enemies, but Psalm 38 is a prayer concerned with an enemy within—sin. Often your inclination when overcome by sin is to cover it up. David, however, knew that nothing is hidden from God. Instead of trying to cover things up, he turned to God in prayer. He laid his struggle open before God.

This is the beauty of having a personal devotion time. Things hidden away in the recesses of your heart and mind can be opened up to God, the One who can heal every wound and minister to every need.

1–3.   **How has communicating with the Lord recently met an emotional need or helped you to overcome a hurt?**

A third example is Psalm 88:9. Grief will affect you at some time or another. In this passage, you can see that the Psalmist dealt with his grief by communicating with God. He called on the Lord every day and spread out his hands before the One he loved.

1–4. *Think back to a time you were really grieving, possibly over the loss of someone close to you. Did you tell the Lord everything you felt, including any anger or confusion? How did that make a difference in how you felt?*

These passages cover a wide range of human problems—difficulties imposed on you by outside circumstances, your own failures that haunt you, and grief that numbs you. You need help when you face these and other anxieties. That help can come from the Lord. But you must first establish the line of communication with Him.

This is what daily devotions are about. Instead of waiting for a crisis to occur before hastily entering God's presence with a plea for help, the person who regularly practices daily devotions is already in the habit of coming before God with his or her needs.

Communicating with God calls for more than calling out to Him. Communication is two way. Speaking of his habit of morning prayers, David said that after he presented his requests before the Lord, he expectantly waited for the answer (Psalm 5:3).

1–5.   *In your devotions, who does most of the talking—you or God? How can you improve your communication with Him so that it is truly two way?*

Waiting on God is an expression of faith. You do not have to wait wondering if God is going to answer; you can wait in anticipation of what that answer will be (Psalm 130:5,6).

1–6.   *It is difficult for some Christians trust that God responds when they share with Him. Why do you think this is so?*

God's Word is an important part of hearing from Him. Read until you sense the Spirit speaking, then listen.

1–7.   *How has God used a Bible verse or story to speak to you?*

The importance of a daily time with God can hardly be overstated. In fact, Paul taught believers to devote themselves to it (Colossians 4:2). Personal devotions must be more than an every-once-in-a-while experience. They must be daily.

Worshiping God The King

Personal devotions also give you a time for worship. In Psalm 63:2–4, David took time to glorify God. He had seen the magnificent works that God had done; he had seen God's power and glory displayed. He responded by praising God and lifting his hands (verses 3,4).

You can do no less. God is working in your life. His power and glory are still being displayed around the world. For those acts, you must praise Him. Such a response to God is sensible as well as spiritual. Once you catch a glimpse of God's character, the logical response to such an awe-inspiring experience is worship.

1–8. *What aspect of God really "wows" you? Write your own psalm of praise, thanking God for being exactly like He is.*

In Psalm 92:1, the writer called worship "good," or fitting. The reasons are expressed in verses 4 and 5. God has done so much for you. How can you hold back praise that rightfully belongs to Him? How can you enter God's presence, gain an awareness of such attributes, and not be inspired to worship?

Worship has a natural place in your devotional life. You do well, then, to heed David's call to worship in Psalm 145:1–3. You must make worship, along with prayer and Bible reading, a daily part of your life. After all, "great is the Lord and most worthy of praise" (Psalm 145:3).

Chapter Review

Some things you cannot afford to do and other things you cannot afford to do without. If you consider the purpose of personal devotions, they naturally fall in the second category. You simply cannot afford to neglect them. The same is true with your relationship with God. If you want to draw closer to Him, you must spend time with Him.

1–9.   *Think of a special relationship in your own life. How would a lack of time spent together affect your relationship?*

If you currently do not have a regular time for devotions, start one. Take time each day to communicate with God. Take your troubles to Him and listen for His response.

If you do have a devotional time each day, look for ways to improve it. You will find that your relationship with the Lord will grow deeper and become more intimate as you seek to know Him better.

Making Time For Prayer

Can you think of something that has been accomplished because people prayed? Look in your Bible and you will see amazing examples of answered prayers—the dead raised to life, future events revealed, the sick healed. Someone has said "the devil trembles when the weakest saint gets on his knees." There is no greater resource at your disposal than prayer.

This chapter will help you to focus on the importance of prayer. It is hoped that once you have considered this, you will find yourself actively making time to pray.

Developing A Prayer Life

2–1.   How would you define prayer?

The Bible is clear on what prayer is not. In Matthew 6:5–8, Jesus used the Pharisees, Israel's strict religious leaders, and pagans as examples of the kinds of prayer God does not honor. God does not want you to seek to impress others with your prayers. Neither is He concerned with the length of your prayers nor how loudly you pray. Instead, God desires you to come to Him with a sincere heart.

So what is God's view of prayer? First, it is taking your deepest personal needs to the Lord. That is what Paul was talking about in Philippians 4:6,7. God does not want to see you worry about your problems. He wants to help you through them.

2–2.   What are some needs you have that you could present to the Lord in prayer?

The scope of prayer is broad enough to meet any need you face. If you depend on your personal resources, you may well have reason to worry. But when you turn to God through prayer, your resources become as unlimited as He is. Then, you can experience the result described in verse 7—a peace "which transcends all understanding."

Prayer even allows you to reach beyond yourself and your personal needs. It allows you to reach out to others as well. In 1 Timothy 2:1,2, Paul urged Timothy to pray for "everyone" (verse 1). Within the scope of that term, Paul included "kings and all those in authority" (verse 2). Just think of it: when you slip away to your private place of prayer each day, you have the ability to influence governmental leaders. In the process, you are blessed by your intercession, because prayer has the ability to stabilize the government, which in turn provides security and peace.

2–3.   Who are some others you could pray for regularly?

Changing Circumstances

What happens when people pray? Does anything really happen? Do circumstances really change? The Bible gives numerous examples to answer these questions.

Consider the Hebrew Daniel's experience as recorded in Daniel 10:12–19. Troubled by a vision he had seen, Daniel turned to God (verses 1–3). Verses 12–19 point out several significant things about prayer.

It is interesting to note the reason that Daniel had to wait so long for his prayer to be answered. The Lord had sought to answer his prayer immediately, but the messenger had been delayed. You must not become discouraged when answers to prayer seem slow in coming; you must continue to bring your requests to the Lord.

Notice, also, that Daniel expressed his weakness in prayer (verse 17). The angel's response was to touch him, giving him the power he needed to continue (verses 18,19). You may sometimes feel too weak to pray. Like Daniel, however, you can renew your strength through the act of prayer itself.

2–4. *Write about a time you almost gave up praying, but found the strength to continue through God and saw your prayers answered.*

Prayer changed things for Daniel: his understanding of God's plan broadened and his own strength increased. As someone has said, "Prayer changes things—even me."

Next, consider Peter's prison experience (Acts 12:5–7). As Peter suffered in prison, the church was busy praying for him (verse 5). As a result of those prayers, a miracle took place. Peter was delivered from the jail and escorted by an angel to the gate of the city. Prayer can move God to lift you above your circumstances.

2–5. *What seemingly impossible need does someone you know have? Pray about it daily for the next week.*

Finally, consider Paul and Silas' imprisonment in Acts 16:22–26. These two missionaries had suffered a great deal. A mob had formed among the very people they were trying to reach with the gospel. As a result, Paul and Silas were flogged, imprisoned, and placed in the innermost part of the jail. They were placed in stocks. Hope seemed to be gone.

But Paul and Silas did not give up hope. Instead they prayed and sang praises to God. The effect of their prayer was dramatic: a "violent earthquake" shook the jail so violently that "the prison doors flew open, and everybody's chains came loose" (verse 26).

When you are forced to face adverse circumstances, you may feel helpless in yourself. Prayer, however, lifts you above your circumstances, changing adversity so it works in your favor and glorifies God.

Having Confidence

Now you know why you need to pray, but you must also consider how you should pray—with confidence. In Matthew 7:7–11, Jesus related the reason you can have confidence: "everyone who asks receives." Your first concern in making requests must be God's will, not your personal preferences. But the rule still stands: asked prayers are answered prayers.

2–6.   *According to this passage, upon whose character is the believer's confidence in prayer based—his own or God's? Why is this distinction so important?*

If your confidence were based on what you have earned, you would do better to give up praying completely, because there is no way you can pray with confidence if receiving an answer depends on your own character. This passage makes it very clear that the loving character of God, and nothing else, is the basis for your confidence in prayer (verse 11).

Couple this passage with another that emphasizes the nature of the One to whom you pray. In Hebrews 4:14–16, Jesus is described as someone who understands your situation and is sympathetic to your needs.

Have you ever tried to share a problem with someone you knew had little or no understanding of your situation? You knew that person could not possibly know what you were going through or how you were feeling. That is why it is important for you to remember that Jesus has gone through the same difficulties you have. He understands your needs. He knows why you are hurting. You do not need to be shy or hesitant in presenting your needs to Him. He understands because He has been there! You can come before His throne confidently because you know that the One to whom you are coming knows exactly how you feel.

2–7.   What do Jesus' empathy and genuine compassion for your needs mean to you personally when you pray?

You can also be confident that God listens to your sincere prayers (1 John 5:14,15). It is important to remember this does not include your selfish ambitions. God does not hear the prayer that is offered with a wrong motive. But He will hear and answer those who come to Him with pure motives.

2–8.   Think of a time you prayed selfishly for something to happen that was probably not God's will. What happened?

Always remember to pray selflessly if you want to pray with power. When you include prayer in your devotional time, you are able to tap into a resource that takes you beyond your limitations. You link yourself to the One whose power and ability are unsurpassed.

Chapter Review

Think for a moment of the routines that are a part of your life. What are some of the things that you do on a regular basis? Imagine leaving out one of these aspects of your life. Imagine sleeping all day, instead of waking up. Imagine not eating day after day, or not expressing care to those around you. How empty life would be! These patterns and customs may be ordinary, but they are vital.

If you find yourself so pressed for time that you think you can no longer take any significant time to pray, you probably need to reconsider just how important prayer is to you. Taking time to talk with the Lord must be high on your list of priorities.

2–9. How could you rearrange your daily schedule or eliminate optional activities so that you have time to pray?

Prayer must become important to every believer. It cannot be merely something you use when necessary. It must be just as much a part of your everyday life as waking and eating. Far from an empty routine, prayer is an absolute necessity that must be a consistent part of your living.

Take time to examine your own devotional life. If it includes prayer, take various ideas from biblical prayers to make it better. If prayer is lacking from your daily routine, find a time to pray. Start with a few minutes and gradually increase. Your relationship with Christ can only become more fulfilling.

Praying God's Way

If you learned the Lord's Prayer when you were a child, you probably memorized it word for word. As is often the case with well-known passages, you may know the words so well that you sometimes forget to pay attention to the real meaning behind them. Despite this tendency, the Lord's Prayer is eternally relevant. These magnificent words of Jesus have a higher purpose than being admired for their beauty or repeated mechanically.

Jesus used the Lord's Prayer to guide His disciples into a more solid relationship with His Father. His model prayer can grow more proficient in your own prayer life. When you look at the principles and the words Jesus taught, you will see how your prayers can follow guidelines that will result in dynamic spiritual growth.

Giving God Reverence

Luke recorded the request of one of Jesus' disciples: "Lord, teach us to pray, as John also taught his disciples" (Luke 11:1). The disciples had numerous opportunities to witness the effectiveness of Jesus' prayers demonstrated under a variety of circumstances. They recognized Jesus' special relationship to God, and they wanted to imitate the qualities in His life that allowed Him such access to heaven's provision.

3–1.   **What do you want to learn from the Lord's Prayer which could deepen your prayer life?**

Prayer, in itself, was a common practice. The Jews were historically a people of prayer, but they had allowed prayer to become a means of public display (see Matthew 6:5). Jesus' lessons in prayer made it clear that prayer is not to be used to earn spiritual recognition. Prayer is a vital communication link between earthly children and their Heavenly Father—a means of nourishing a vital spiritual relationship.

3–2.   **What are your prayers like—speeches or conversations? How is the way you typically pray affecting your relationship with the Lord?**

Those mature Christians whom you regard with respect as "prayer warriors" are just everyday believers who have learned to apply Jesus' principles of prayer. They have developed a deep understanding of their relationship to God, as well as their place within His will. Their submission to Him has resulted in an effective prayer life. All believers—including you—are offered the same opportunity.

The first part of Jesus' teaching on prayer involved the sample prayer that has come to be known as the Lord's Prayer. Read this prayer as recorded in Luke 11:2–4.

Notice that Jesus called God "Father." Once you have joined God's family, you can confidently go to Him as your Heavenly Father. You can commune with God with the same intimacy and confidence you enjoy with a special relative or friend. Your confidence, however, is to be tempered by your reverence for God's holiness. The phrase "Hallowed be Thy name" recognizes this unchanging characteristic of God.

3–3.   Where do you think the balance is between being close to God and respecting His incredible power and authority?

In recent years, some popular teaching on prayer has left the impression that God wants to be your "buddy." Some have taken this to mean that they can approach God any way they desire. In many cases, this has produced an irreverent attitude. Certainly, God wants to share in your life; He desires to be your Friend and longs to be a part of everything you do. However, He is still God. If you pray as Jesus prayed, you must honor the Lord and give Him all the respect He deserves.

Part of this respect is recognizing your need to submit to God's will. In the version of the prayer recorded in Matthew 6 and in some manuscripts of Luke 11:2, Jesus prayed that God's will would be performed on earth as completely as it is in heaven. This is certainly an important aspect of the coming of the Lord's kingdom, since His kingdom is everywhere His will is obeyed.

3–4.   *How much do you think your personal obedience to God's will can help or hinder the coming of God's kingdom?*

Presenting Your Petitions

The next section of Jesus' prayer—Luke 11:3,4—offers guidelines on petitioning God with your needs. Jesus addressed both physical and spiritual needs in His prayer.

To represent the variety of physical needs you experience, Jesus referred to "daily bread" (verse 3). Both words are important: "bread" addresses the actual need and "daily" reminds you one cannot live on yesterday's answered prayers.

Each day you need to recognize your complete dependence on His provision. It is easy, especially in a society accustomed to plenty, to take for granted things like climate-controlled homes, well-stocked grocery stores, and readily available clothing. You must watch that these blessings do not lull you into a false confidence in your own environment. God remains the true Source of everything you enjoy.

3–5.   List some basic needs you know God has met and thank Him for doing so.

Jesus next addressed spiritual needs (verse 4). You must make petition for the forgiveness of your sins and commit yourself to forgiving others who have wronged you. Besides addressing sins already committed, Jesus taught that you can ask God for spiritual protection when faced with challenges to your faith. God will keep you safe in the midst of the most severe temptations if you will put your trust in Him.

3–6.   Write a prayer asking God to help you resist and overcome a particular temptation you have been giving in to frequently.

Praying With Persistence

After He showed His disciples an example prayer, Jesus continued His teaching on prayer with some general guidelines (Luke 11:5–10). Using a parable, He taught the disciples the importance of exercising their faith through persistent prayer. There are those who would teach that you can always pray just once and expect an immediate answer. Jesus' parable teaches otherwise.

In the story, a man found himself accepting a midnight guest and having nothing to feed him. Embarrassed, the host went immediately to his neighbor to borrow bread, only to be turned down. At his persistence, the reluctant neighbor gave in and loaned him the bread.

Jesus was careful to explain that the reason the neighbor responded was not because of friendship custom, or because he was a good neighbor. Instead, he responded because of the man's persistence. Jesus was not suggesting that God is put off by your requests. He was contrasting God's love with the neighbor's indignation. If the neighbor, as irritated as he was, was willing to meet a need, how much more willing must God be to meet the needs of His own beloved children?

3–7.   *What have you been praying about and are discouraged that you do not have the answer yet? How has this parable encouraged you?*

Jesus concluded this portion of His lesson by giving the disciples a promise: "Ask and it will be given to you; seek and you will find; knock and the door will be opened to you" (verse 9). This verse implies that you are continually asking, seeking, and knocking. It also implies that if you continue to do these things, you have the promise of God's response.

Trusting God For The Answer

In Luke 11:11–13, Jesus emphasized again the importance of your family relationship with God. You can approach the Father in full confidence that He will give you your requests in accordance with what is needful in your life.

Jesus drew several contrasts to illustrate this truth. He asked His listeners to think what they would do if one of their children requested a simple food, such as bread, fish, or an egg. Certainly, the parents would not respond by giving them a stone, a serpent, or a scorpion! Their forefathers had told them stories about the serpent in the wilderness and the scorpions that invaded Israel's camps. Serpents and scorpions were symbols of hurt, harm, and danger. No good father would even think of responding to his child's request in this manner.

3–8.   *You (or someone you know) may not have had good parents who provided for your needs. How has this affected the way you view your Heavenly Father?*

Jesus then made a powerful comparison. If a human, who is by nature evil, would not reject his child's needs, then how much more will God, who loves and desires only the best for His people, give good things to them when they pray. Although Jesus identified this "good gift" as the Holy Spirit, the promise covers all that you will ever need.

It seems that at times people have made prayer too hard. Some of the terminology used to describe prayer, such as "bombarding heaven" and "struggling in travail," reinforces the idea that prayer is battling with God to get your way. But as this chapter has shown, prayer is meant to be a positive experience filled with spiritual blessings—you and the Lord battling together to accomplish what He wants.

Chapter Review

The Lord's Prayer and His teaching on the subject in Luke 11:1–12 can give you wonderful insight into how God views prayer. According to Jesus, prayer is you confidently yet humbly yielding all concerns, whether physical or spiritual, to the Lord so you and He can cooperate in seeing those concerns addressed. Regardless of how other people have treated you, you can be sure that God will treat you fairly, providing just the answer you need.

3–9.   *What have you learned about prayer from this chapter that has helped you the most? How will it change the way you pray?*

Part Two

Exploring God's Word

When someone talks about reading the Bible, what comes to your mind? Do you think of struggling to keep your eyes open as you wander through old stories and endless lists of commands? Or do your eyes light up thinking of the latest wonderful thing you learned when reading the Bible—maybe something about God and what He desires to see in you? The first thing you think of when Bible study is mentioned says a lot about what you are putting into reading Scripture and what you have been getting out of it.

This unit can open your mind and heart to the possibilities of Bible study. There are different ways you can read God's Word, three of which are explained in the next few chapters. No matter which method you use—devotional, topical, or systematic—studying the Bible can yield its own treasures if you invest a little time and effort. And, as you will find, this source of treasure is inexhaustible.

Letting God Speak Through His Word

You live in a very health conscious society. People keep track of calories, cholesterol, fat, and sodium. But of all the people who work hard to maintain healthy bodies, how many think about their spiritual health?

Just as eating the right foods is important for physical health, "eating" the right mix and amount of spiritual "food" is important if you want a strong and firm spirit. Where do you get this necessary spiritual food? Pop psychology is junk food, low in spiritual nutrition and high in humanistic "fat." It is only as you study God's Word daily that you will find the nourishment you need for a healthy spiritual life. You can tap into those nutrients through devotional Bible study.

Receiving From The Word

Of all the Bible study methods, the devotional method is probably the most popular. Other types of study focus on learning a doctrine or studying a biblical book. Although at times these things may be the focus of devotional Bible study, one of its main purposes is receiving encouragement and spiritual strength for everyday living. The focus is always toward what you can learn from a Bible verse or passage that can immediately be applied to your current situation.

4–1.   *Think of a time you were really encouraged by a Bible verse or story. What did you learn from it that blessed you?*

> Esther 4:16 Esther fasted
> for three days and three nights
> (she commanded the fast.)
>
> Est 4:3 Mordecai fasted and prayed
> as well as those Jews who heard
> the decree. (I can apply the scripture
> to my life and receive results

You may come to devotions with a decision weighing on your mind. Studying the Bible devotionally can guide you in making these decisions. As you meditate on God's Word, the Holy Spirit can provide the direction you need.

4–2.   *How has God used a Bible verse or story to help you make a decision? How did He do that?*

> Psalm 37:25 I have been young
> and now am old; yet I have I not
> seen the righteous forsaken, nor his seed
> begging bread. This verse of scripture
> has help me to gain faith and believe God
> in more areas.

Another goal of devotional study is applying the Bible to lifestyle characteristics. As you meditate on the portion of Scripture you have chosen for study, God will use it to speak to you concerning habits, attitudes, and actions that need changing.

4–3. *In what area of your lifestyle has God been challenging you lately when you read the Bible?*

Continuing
to live a life of meditation and application
to accomplish God's will and purpose
for my life. Joshua 1:8, Psalm 1:2-3

I am constantly reminded of God's existence and presence in
Creation, His word is truth and helps me to remember where I
came from, where I am now and where I'm going. Also I'm
reminded that I serve a Holy God and he requires me to be holy.

Reflecting On Important Truths

The best way to understand how devotional Bible study works and what you can gain from it is to practice it. You will use Psalm 19 as the portion of Scripture for this devotional study. Take your Bible and read the entire psalm.

Psalm 104:N

4–4. *What do you see in this psalm that will help you in your daily walk with the Lord?*

The poem (psalm) begins with the heavens, centers on the
Word, and culminates in the heart of the servant
of God. ① a celebration of the greatness of God's
Creation V1-6, ② a celebration of the purity of the
word of God V7-11, ③ a contemplation of the life of
the person of God V12-14.

One of the important aspects of the devotional study is meditating on what you read. You may be uncomfortable with the term *meditation* in light of the focus it receives from some mystical religions. However, their ideas and methods of meditation are far different from the believer's meditation on God's Word. Instead of repeating a mantra to achieve divine

The Sun illuminates God's Creation and provides a constant source of heat and light and all of Creation is touched by it.

consciousness, you are to carefully contemplate God's Word to enrich your understanding of it.

4–5. **Meditate on Psalm 19:1–6, then write down what you have learned about God through His creation.**

I have learned that God has a plan and a purpose for all of creation. He has infinite knowledge. John 1:3 All things were made by him; and without him was not anything made that was made. Rev 4:11 Thou art worthy O to receive glory and honour and power: for thou hast created all things, and for thy pleasure they are and were created.

4–6. **Now concentrate on verses 7–11 for a while. How do David's descriptions of God's Word portray its different aspects?** There is no flaws in God's law and it leads every person to Christ. The fool may obtain wisdom through God's Word.

Six words for the law - law, testimony, statutes, commandment, fear, and judgment
Six evaluations - perfect, sure, right, pure, clean, and true. (results of the law - Converting the soul, making wise the simple, rejoicing the heart, enlightening the eyes, enduring forever, righteous altogether)

4–7. **How did studying God's Word help David in daily living?** Psalm 119

It allowed him to be in constant fellowship with God, to see God for who he is, and measure and examine his life in accordance with the Word of God. It provided David with the key to wisdom, joy, and fellowship with God here, and the assurance of eternal life.

Relating Bible Principles To Life

After you have reflected on the passage, it is time to apply what you have learned to life. The end goal of devotional study is a changed life. One of this type of study's benefits is encouragement and strength for daily living.

4–8. *What encouragement did you receive from your increased understanding of God and His wisdom and power?*

God is Sovereign, the Creator of all things, His word takes precedence it is the final authority, When I obey God's word it blesses my life. When I fall short of God's word He deals with me accordingly and Puts me back where I belong.

As you discover verses that are especially meaningful to you, it is good to commit them to memory. Many people have a regular system for memorizing God's Word during their devotional time. When you memorize God's Word, you can meditate on it wherever you are even if you do not have a Bible with you.

4–9. *What did you discover about God's Word that can help you make decisions?*

The law of the Lord is perfect Converting the soul: the testimony of the Lord is sure, making wise the simple.

As you spend time meditating on God's Word, the Holy Spirit may speak to you about changes that need to take place in your life. Look at David's response to God concerning the conduct of his life in Psalm 19:12–14.

4–10. **How do you think David was able to discern his errors? And what part did the Word play in his being able to do this?**

David examined himself in the light of God's holiness and he did this through the study of God's word. This allowed him to judge himself outwardly as well as inwardly and the areas he was not aware of.

4–11. **According to verse 14, why are the things that you think about important?**

Because if we are thinking about things contrary to God's word they will lead us away from God. So David wanted his thought and speech to line up and be pleasing to God

4–12. **What steps will you take to see that the prayer of verse 14 is fulfilled in your life?**

Continue to pray be open and honest with God and examine myself as David did and ask God to help my thought and my speech to line up with his will and his word.

Chapter Review

If you did not establish a consistent time of daily devotions after reading this book's first chapter, make plans to begin this week. Set a specific time each day, then stick to it. If you miss your appointed time, do not give up. Have your devotions and try to keep your appointment with God's Word the next day.

Allow your devotional studies of the Bible to mature you spiritually. You are reading, not so you can say you have read the Bible in a certain time period, but so that you can grow.

4–13. *How has this chapter taught you to apply what you read in the Bible to your spiritual development?*

Also let what you learn from Scripture help you reach out to others. These people include loved ones, coworkers, and other spiritually needy people God brings your way.

4–14. *What are some ways you can share with a friend what the Lord has recently taught you from His Word?*

Studying the Bible topically teaches you what God thinks about most topics.

5

Learning God's View On A Subject

Matthew Henry Pulpit Commentary

Have you ever needed a biblical answer to a problem you were facing? If you have been a Christian for any length of time, you probably answered, "Yes." But how do you go about finding biblical answers for life's challenges? One of the best ways to find these answers is through the topical Bible study method.

Selected passages will be used in this chapter to show you how to follow a topic through the Bible and apply it to your life—Isaiah 28:11,12; Joel 2:28–32; Matthew 3:11,12; Luke 11:9–13; 24:49; John 7:37–39; Acts 1:7,8; 2:1–4; 8:14–19; 9:17–19; 10:44–48; and 19:1–7. The steps described in this study can be used to study any Bible topic. Become familiar with them, and a whole new approach to Bible study will become open to you.

Choosing Your Focus

A multitude of topics can be considered in a topical Bible study. Deciding on a topic is the first step in your study. While this may sound obvious, just the process of choosing a topic can be instructive. Topics may range from finding answers to a problem to studying one of the doctrines of the Bible.

5–1.   Write down some topics that interest you and that could be studied in the Bible.

1. Christian Conduct

2. How did Jesus live OR The life Of Jesus

3. The role Of the Holy Spirit

How to be SAved OR How does One acquire Salvation

There are some things to consider that will help you gain the most benefit from this method. When starting a topical study, make sure you choose a topic narrow enough to be studied easily. Studying broader topics can be discouraging because of the amount of material you will discover. (You can tackle broader topics as your experience in this Bible study method increases.) Also, make sure you do a thorough study. To only study a portion of the topic may result in a biased and unbiblical view.

This chapter study will focus on the baptism in the Holy Spirit. This topic would fit within a larger topical study on the person of the Holy Spirit. To get an idea of how broad a general study of the Spirit would be, take a few moments and look up "Holy Spirit" in an exhaustive concordance or the concordance at the back of your Bible. You will find many verses that mention the Spirit. These and many others could be used to study the doctrine of the Holy Spirit in the Bible.

After the topic has been chosen, you will need to list all of the verses that contain any reference to your topic. The place to start is your previous familiarization with Scripture. Write all of the verses you can recall that deal with your chosen topic. After this is done, it is time to turn to some useful tools in Bible study.

As already mentioned, one of the basic tools for any type of Bible study is a concordance. Many Bibles have a small concordance in the back which can be helpful. But in order to find all of the passages related to a topic, an exhaustive concordance is a must.

Another helpful tool is the cross-reference system in the margins of many Bibles. Cross-referencing similar topics helps locate further verses.

Topical Bibles are also helpful. These Bibles contain an extensive list of passages arranged by topics. They may not list every verse needed for your study, but they can provide another excellent place to start.

With today's technology, many computer Bible programs will do word and phrase searches. Not only does this speed up your search, the phrase search may be extremely helpful in locating passages strongly tied to your topic.

5–2. *Of the topical study resources listed above, which ones do you have already? Which ones could you get in the near future?*

NIV
Illustrated Dictionary
Bible Study
Nelson's

Cross reference Bible
Exhaustive Concordance
Thompson Chain Reference Bible
Complete Expository Dictionary
Bible from 26 Translations
Contemporary Bible

In the future I can get a computer Bible program

After you have listed all the Scriptures related to your topic, you need to organize them into subtopics or categories. By doing this, you will discover different aspects of your topic. This will also place the verses in smaller, more manageable segments.

Look at the verses mentioned at the beginning of this chapter—Isaiah 28:11,12; Joel 2:28–32; Matthew 3:11,12; Luke 11:9–13; 24:49; John 7:37–39; Acts 1:7,8; 2:1–4; 8:14–19; 9:17–19; 10:44–48; and 19:1–7.

5–3. *These passages can be divided into several categories. Take a few minutes to read each passage and then group all similar verses into titled categories.*

-

-

-

Analyzing The Passages

After you have listed all the verses related to your topic in separate categories, it is time to examine these passages. The first step is to make some general observations about each verse. Write basic facts you discover as you read each verse. Some important things to look for are people and their reactions to situations, places, dates, events, and important words. There are several ways to record these observations. One way is to write the verse at the top of a sheet of paper and write your observations on this sheet. You can also develop charts that organize your findings in the categories mentioned above.

5–4. Reread these passages—Acts 1:7,8; 2:1–4; 8:14–19; 9:17–19; 10:44–48; and 19:1–7. Make a list of observations you make as you read.

After you have listed all your observations, you can begin to analyze each passage. There are several things to keep in mind when doing this. First, you must remember to study each passage in its context. In a topical study, there might only be one verse in a chapter that deals with your subject. But the surrounding verses will have an effect on the way that verse is interpreted. Verses taken out of their contexts can take on a whole different meaning than that intended by the original writer.

the 4:14 / it fulfills / riches

5–5. How might taking topical verses out of their original contexts affect your entire topical study?

Mt 19:24 And again I say unto
Mk 10:25 you, That ~~a rich man~~ it is
Lk 18:25 easier for a camel to go through
the eye of a needle, than for a rich
man to enter into the kingdom of
God. (Luke 18:22-25 (v24) And when Jesus
saw that he was very sorrowful

Second, make sure you study each passage independently of all other passages. There can be a temptation to look at

He said, How hardly shall they that have
riches enter into the kingdom of God!

parallel passages, noting similarities and differences. This step will come later. In the meantime, it is important to let each passage speak for itself.

When analyzing a passage, six important questions need to be asked—*When? Who? What? Where? Why?* and *How?* Asking these types of questions where applicable will help you focus your search for the fullest understanding of any particular passage.

There are several resources that can be used in analyzing Scripture. A good commentary is invaluable. Not only will it help you understand your passage, it will also list alternative interpretations of difficult passages.

Researching a topic includes word studies, but goes beyond the analysis of the words in the topic. Both synonyms and antonyms need to be considered. Word study books are very helpful research tools. You do not have to be a Greek or Hebrew scholar to take advantage of some of these books that are available.

Making Personal Application

Any type of Bible study is not complete until personal application is made to your life. If you began a study looking for a scriptural answer to a problem, how are you going to respond to your results? If you have studied a doctrine of Scripture, how is this newly acquired knowledge going to make a difference in your life?

5–6.   *This chapter focused on the baptism in the Holy Spirit. How did the information you discovered affect your life?*

5–7.   *How does God's purpose for giving the Baptism impact
       you?*

5–8.   *What further steps do you need to take to fully apply the
       results of your study to your life?*

When pondering the application of a passage of Scripture
to your life, do not just rely on your ability to think critically
and analytically. Ask the Holy Spirit to speak to your heart
and show you where your life needs to change in order to
conform to the standards of God's Word. He is the Spirit of
Truth, and He will be faithful to teach you all things (see
John 14:17,26).

Chapter Review

The topical Bible study method can be one of the most
valuable methods you will ever learn. You can find the answer

to almost any problem or need by using this method. This is a straightforward way of studying the Bible that will prove increasingly rewarding as you invest time and effort in it.

Begin to develop a topical Bible study this week. From the list you created at the beginning of this chapter, choose a topic that interests you. Do the research needed to discover all the verses dealing with this topic and analyze each one. Then, apply the truths you have discovered to your life, and let God transform you by His Word.

Studying Inductively

Have you ever begun a study of one of the books of the Bible only to become overwhelmed by details? Many Christians have had this experience. This chapter will help you learn how to study a biblical book using the inductive method. This method helps you take a book of the Bible and study it thoroughly step-by-step.

A key to avoiding discouragement in any Bible study method is to start simply. This is especially true for a more involved process like the inductive method. This week's study will focus on the Book of Jude. It has been called "Jude's half sheet of notebook paper" because of its short length. But this book has much to teach you about the believer's faithfulness to God's Word. Before you continue in this chapter, read the Book of Jude.

Examining The Passage

One of the best ways to obtain knowledge of the Bible is to study it book by book. When you study a book of the Bible, you study in a systematic manner. You can discover doctrines in the Bible in the context of one book as opposed to a topical study in which a doctrine is researched through the entire Bible.

The first step in studying a book of the Bible is to read it through in one sitting, if possible. Many books of the New Testament can be read in 30 minutes to an hour. The longer books of the Bible will take two or three sittings.

During your research, you will need to discover the overall purpose of the book. Do this for the Book of Jude. This is a very important foundational step that cannot be bypassed.

6–1. *Why do you think Jude wrote this particular letter? To whom did he write it?*

Almost every book of the Bible has a theme and a key verse. Discovering these things will help you understand the purpose behind the writing of that book. When the purpose has been discovered, you begin to see how everything that was written fits together.

Read the Book of Jude again. To find the theme, review why it seems he wrote the letter. Also try to discover the one verse that sums up the purpose of this letter.

6–2. *Write out the verse that seems to contain Jude's theme.*

After these basic items have been discovered, the next step is to determine the structure of the book by outlining it. Most books can be outlined easily. An outline is valuable because it helps you see the progression of the author's thought.

The easiest way to begin outlining an epistle, or biblical letter, is to look for the opening and ending sections. Then you can find the other main points by looking for major shifts in the author's thought in the body of the book.

6–3.   *Jude contains several main points, including the opening and closing sections. Record them in the space below.*

-
-
-
-
-
-
-

After the main points have been discovered, subpoints within them can be outlined in a similar manner. You can continue to outline subpoints and sub-subpoints of the Book of Jude on a separate sheet of paper.

With an established outline, it is time to begin looking for details in order to discover what the author said. This involves reading the text carefully and writing down anything that seems important.

6–4.   *Select a main point in the Book of Jude and read its verses carefully. Look for descriptions of people, their actions, God's response, and anything else you feel is important.*

Interpreting The Meaning

After discovering what the author said, the next step is to discover what he meant. Study his words and phrases. As you do, ask yourself: "Why did the author use those particular words and phrases?" You do not need to be a biblical languages scholar to do this. Biblical word study books, the dictionary, and various translations of the Bible can help you.

6–5.   *Pick several key words or phrases in the main point you selected. What do you think they mean?*

Another important part of understanding the author's meaning is realizing the book's historical context. Most New

Testament epistles are known as occasional documents: there was a specific occasion that prompted the writing of each of these apostolic letters—an interpersonal problem, a doctrinal question, a troubling circumstance, or the need for a warning or clarification.

Knowing a little about the political, geographic, and social history surrounding the writing of a book can broaden your understanding of it. A study Bible or Bible encyclopedia or dictionary can help you find this information.

6–6.   *If you have these study tools, look through them for clues about the situation behind the Book of Jude. Also look for clues in the letter itself. What did you find out?*

It is now time to summarize what you have discovered with brief questions based on the six interrogatives and their answers. You can use a good commentary or study Bible to help you answer your questions fully.

6–7.   *Write out questions (and their answers) about Jude's letter that will help you understand it better.*

Who...

What...

When...

Where...

Why...

How...

Applying The Biblical Truth

No Bible study is complete until what you have learned is applied to your life. Remember, the goal of Bible study is not just to gain biblical knowledge. The end result of your study should be to grow in spiritual maturity. The first step in this portion of the study is to discover the historical application of the book. In other words, what did Jude want his readers to learn from his letter? After this, it is time to look for any principles that will apply to your life.

Look at Jude 3,4. The word Jude used for "contend" is a word commonly used in athletic competition. It has the idea of aggressive pursuit to win an athletic contest. The word "faith" describes the sound doctrine that was the basis for all biblical teaching and preaching in the Early Church. Jude asked his readers to "contend for the faith."

6–8.   *Given the meaning of "contend" and "faith," what was Jude asking his recipients to do?*

Now that you have discovered what this verse probably meant to these believers, it is time to determine the significance to your own life. "The faith" would be the equivalent of sound biblical doctrine.

6–9. *What would you first need to do to determine what sound doctrine was? Before you contend for sound doctrine, what role would it need to play in your life?*

As you answer these and other questions concerning what you have learned in your study of Jude, you will be able to apply this knowledge to your spiritual life.

Sometimes what was written in a passage has to do only with the specific situation that was being addressed in that letter. In order for you to have a proper interpretation and develop the right application, this situation must be discovered. But keep in mind, even if a passage has a specific application only to the original audience, there are still principles for you to consider. All Scripture has principles that can be applied to life.

6–10. *What general principles have you learned from Jude?*

Chapter Review

Studying God's Word inductively requires an investment of time. Although other methods generally focus on shorter passages, this method encompasses whole books or larger sections of books. But the time spent in this type of study is invaluable.

Read through Jude again. Look at Jude's description of false teachers and their destruction. Examine his instructions to believers concerning their own faith. Then observe God's faithfulness to His own who faithfully serve Him.

6–11. *Evaluate your own life in light of your study of Jude. What false ideas promoted by the world challenge your faith?*

6–12. *What steps can you take to hold onto God's truth and continue maturing spiritually in spite of these challenges?*

Part Three

Living In God's Will

Finding and obeying God's will is simultaneously simple and complex. It is theoretically simple, the most basic guide to living a life that pleases the Lord. If you follow the Lord's will, no matter how you feel about it or whether or not you understand it, you will bring Him joy. And yet finding and obeying God's will is incredibly complex in practice. When faced with a decision, how do you know which option is the will of God? And how can you be sure the main influence in your decision to choose one option over another is the Lord's will and not your own?

As you will be reminded in this unit, living in God's will does not have to be as intimidating as it is for many believers. The next two chapters show the importance of your attitude if you are to successfully carry out the will of God. Fear and independence must be replaced with trust and humility. With this foundation in place, chapter 9 reviews specific methods you can use to determine what God's will for you is.

God has a special plan in mind for every believer.

Understanding God's Plan

Religion and spirituality are extremely hot topics today. People are looking, often in the wrong places, for trustworthy answers about the origin of life, its meaning, and what comes after this physical life ends. Of course, the sources of most of the answers people are accepting as true are anything but trustworthy.

Interest in religion is even evident on the World Wide Web. According to one news magazine, a 1996 search of the Web for "Bill Gates" (the head of Microsoft) produced an impressive 25,000 entries. But the same browser found 146,000 entries for "Christ" and 410,000, for "God."

Millions of people are searching for God and for what their lives mean in relation to Him. This chapter will help you find the meaning and value in life while discovering God's purpose for you.

Created For A Purpose

Read Psalm 139:1–16. It is a song of praise celebrating how intimately God knows those He has created.

7–1.   *Have you asked God to help you understand the purpose He has for your life? What might that purpose be?*

The plan God has for you is not the work of a detached being. God knows you better than anyone else (verses 1–6). He is always near you, His child (verses 7–12). He was there with you as you grew in your mother's womb (verses 13–15). Before you were born, He already knew what would happen to you every day of your life (verse 16).

7–2.   *How does realizing that God knows so much about you and your life make you feel?*

Because God knows you better than you know yourself, He knows everything that would be the very best for you. If this is true, is there any area of your life that you can rightly say belongs to you alone and cannot be affected by God's plan for you? Think about this for a minute before continuing with this study. Full surrender to God's purposes for you is a must.

A chalk line is a guide, showing a carpenter where to make a cut. Second Peter 3:9 gives you God's "chalk line," that aspect of His eternal plan that guides all other aspects. He wants everyone to be saved through repentance and belief. The biggest part of God's will for you is your accepting His offer of salvation through Jesus Christ.

7–3. How has being a Christian already affected some of your life's more important decisions—what your interests are, where you went to college, whom you married, etc.?

As a believer, God's overarching plan for you is that you mature spiritually. This is the message of Ephesians 1:4. As it is with all believers, you have been chosen "to be holy and blameless." The development of godly character is one part of God's plan for you that never changes. It is only when you have accepted this as God's first goal for your life that you will succeed in finding His more detailed will.

7–4. Write about a time when knowing that God wants you "to be holy and blameless" affected a major decision you made.

Planned From The Beginning

Having established the starting point of God's plan as your salvation and ongoing, spiritual development, you can begin to understand some of the ways God works out His purpose in your life. It is a delight to know He is at work in you even when you are least aware of it.

According to Romans 8:28,29, God is at work for you in all circumstances. No matter what happens, you have God's promise that He will use even the hard times or seeming wrongs you may suffer to bring about something for your good. Verse 29 indicates this "good" is your becoming like Jesus Christ in character and attitude.

7–5. *Write about a time you endured a horrible situation only to realize later that God made something good come out of it.*

In his letter to the believers in Ephesus, the apostle Paul developed more fully the idea that God guides you through circumstances. Read Ephesians 1:5,11–14. God is completely sovereign: nothing that has happened or will happen to you can take Him by surprise.

Does this mean God's sovereignty allows you no free will? No, God does not predetermine if a person is saved or not. Rather, He freely offers His grace and salvation to all people. Those who resist God's grace freely choose to reject salvation.

Those who accept His offer of salvation and receive His grace do so of their own volition. Then they begin to receive the benefits of salvation God has planned for all who believe.

Notice what your salvation and subsequent spiritual growth does: it brings the Lord praise (verses 6,12, 14). The more you allow God to have His way in your life, the more He will be glorified. In this sense, fulfilling God's plan for your life is an act of worship that exalts Him.

Only God sees the overall picture of human free will and His divinely ordained plan for believers. Humans are limited to seeing life from a day-by-day perspective.

7–6.   *From your limited viewpoint, what have you noticed God doing in and through you lately?*

Attained Over A Lifetime

7–7.   *Read Proverbs 4:18. What does this verse tell you about finding and following God's will in your life?*

Although righteousness is given to you when you are saved, it is also worked out in your life daily. God intensely desires that you be like Christ, but you are not able to achieve perfection all at once. Over time, your life will begin to reflect God's character more and more as you build a relationship with Him.

Psalm 37:23,24 assures you God will uphold you if you walk with Him. He will make your "steps firm" (verse 23), helping you to act in confidence on what you know of His will. The Lord will also keep you from falling (verse 24); whenever you do make mistakes in following Him, He will draw you back to obedience.

7–8. *Think of a time God restored you to himself after a time of disobedience. How has this impacted how you try to live for the Lord today?*

David and Solomon, the men who wrote Psalm 37 and Proverbs 4, were confident that God would be with them as they obeyed His commands. But you have an advantage under the new covenant that neither of these kings enjoyed: you have continual access to God's presence.

According to 2 Corinthians 3:18, you have the Holy Spirit in you at all times, not coming on you occasionally. Moses wore a veil because the glory of God's presence faded (verse 13). You do not need a veil: the glory of God's presence in you is not fading, but increasing.

How do you "reflect the Lord's glory"? As you grow in Christ, your transformed character, attitudes, and actions become evident to your friends and relatives. Your personal growth process has a positive effect on others, just as you can benefit from the maturing of other believers.

7–9.   What do you need to keep this growth constant?

According to Colossians 2:6,7, you must be "rooted" in Christ. Like a plant, you need good soil to grow, with just the right amount of nutrients. Faith is the good soil; thankfulness provides the nourishment you need. As you continue to develop in character over your lifetime, you will achieve God's purpose for you.

Chapter Review

7–10. From this chapter, what have you learned God's plan is for you as a believer?

In order for you to grow in your faith, you must work at seeking God's will in every aspect of life, every day of your life. Anything less than seeking to know and obey Him shortchanges you and dishonors God. He created you for a purpose and He knows you intimately. As you trust Him and center your life on Him, He will fulfill His plan for you.

God wants you to know His will and enjoy the abundant life He has for you. You can be assured He desires the very best for you; such love on God's part demands the very fullest love and trust on your part. How can you experience fullness of trust and love for God? By simply trusting and obeying Him in every way. He will guide you day-by-day in response to your desire to know Him and please Him.

Surrendering To God's Purpose

Is aggressive surrender a contradiction in terms? How can someone surrender and do it aggressively? Ask those who survived the horrors of Nazi concentration camps while friends and family members died all around them.

Dr. Viktor E. Frankl, a Viennese psychiatrist, survived the camps and went on to establish a school of psychotherapy that grew out of his personal suffering and tragedy. Frankl's best-known book, based on his experiences in the camps, is *Man's Search For Meaning*.

In this book, Frankl detailed how he and others survived the German camps. The prisoners actively sought meaning and purpose in the worst of situations. Although they had to surrender to horrible circumstances, they were able to find meaning in them by looking to the future results of their surrendering.

Jesus exemplified surrendering to God's purpose as part of finding and living God's will. The "nevertheless" that Jesus prayed in Gethsemane sums up the aggressive surrender principle. Ask God for guidance in specific matters, but acknowledge that whatever He does is best for your life.

If Dr. Frankl could find hope in a Nazi death camp and if Jesus could see a greater purpose in His death, then you can surely discover hope in your difficult circumstances. This hope can lead you to discover God's purposes for your life. And if you truly believe He wants only the best for you, you will be able to surrender to these purposes, even if doing so leads you through trials.

Ending Your Resistance

8–1. *Which aspects of what might be God's will for your life are unpleasant or scary? Explain your feelings about them.*

If you do not know how to react to the difficulties you will face in fulfilling God's will for you, read Hebrews 12:3,4 to learn how Jesus reacted to His sufferings. Jesus "endured" the sufferings He faced, even when they led to shedding His blood. He did this because He knew His death was part of God's salvation plan.

Has God called on you to die for the gospel or suffer "opposition from sinful men" like Jesus faced? Probably not. So if you are afraid of what might be required of you while doing God's will, think of what Jesus had to endure to follow God's plan for Him. The minor trials you occasionally face are nothing when compared to Jesus' suffering (verse 4). You will be able to endure.

8–2.   How can understanding what Jesus endured to follow
        God's will help you face whatever difficulties will come
        when you pursue God's will for you?

Not all the difficulties you face are suffered because you are
following God's will. Before you complain that surrendering
to God's plan for you will be too hard, remember that some
of the negative circumstances you will have to endure might
be God's way of disciplining you (Hebrews 12:5–11).

Many of the difficulties you face as you serve the Lord
stem from your natural resistance to His will. Because God
loves you, He has to discipline you, attempting to correct
your misbehavior before you make the same errors again
(verses 6). If He were to let you get by with everything, it
would show that He did not care about you at all (verse 8).
But He does care, and so He disciplines you when necessary.

8–3.   Have you ever felt a particular situation was punishment
        from God? Looking back, how have you benefited from
        that discipline?

"No discipline seems pleasant at the time, but painful. Later on, however, it produces a harvest of righteousness and peace for those who have been trained by it" (verse 11). If you allow the Lord to correct your natural resistance to obeying His will, you can achieve the purpose He has for you.

By focusing on God's purpose, you can learn to look at each event and circumstance in your life as part of God's plan. Just as discipline and training sharpens athletes' skills and prepares them for the difficulties of competition, so you can discover new strength and stamina as you align yourself with God's will.

Swallowing Your Pride

The writer of Hebrews stated that the harvest reaped from discipline is "righteousness and peace." But if you do not have the right attitude as you obey God's will, you may harvest self-righteousness. This is the reason the apostle Paul urged believers to follow Jesus' example.

8–4.   *According to Philippians 2:5–11, what was Jesus' attitude as He submitted to God's will?*

Imagine what this was like. The Creator chose to become one of His creatures, just as weak as you are. Even more, He willingly submitted to death by torture for the sake of the very people who would not submit to Him (verse 8). What an example Jesus is to you and other believers as One who put God's will before His own interests.

Jesus had every right to demand worship, but He did not. He simply obeyed, leaving the exalting up to His heavenly Father (verses 9–11). In this, too, you need to follow His example.

8–5. *When have you had to swallow your pride in order to obey the Lord? What did it feel like at the time? How did you feel about it later?*

What can you do to become truly humble like Jesus? Anyone who has tried to do away with pride in his or her life can tell you: humility is difficult to develop. You may feel like the man who said he was so good at being humble that he was proud of it. The truth is, you cannot make yourself humble; it takes a work of God in you.

Second Peter 5:5,6, a well-known passage on humility, links humility to submission to each other, to spiritual leaders, and ultimately to God himself (verse 5). The "proud" whom "God opposes" are the people who refuse to submit to Him or His sovereignty. And "the humble" to whom He "gives grace" are those who willingly submit to His purposes.

Submission and obedience are keys to humility. A literal translation of verse 6 would read: "Be humbled, therefore, under God's mighty hand." You are not able make yourself humble. But by submitting to the Lord, He will humble you.

Does this kind of submission make you God's puppet? No, for just as He exalted Jesus, God longs to exalt you. But you must be humbly submissive before He can do this (verse 6). Nothing will help you surrender to the Lord's will more than knowing that all you have accomplished was possible only because of the grace and favor He has showered on you.

8-6.   *Write a prayer of submission to the Lord, promising Him your undivided loyalty even when what He asks seems too hard or too lowly.*

Enjoying Surrender

8-7.   *Read Proverbs 3:5,6 and Jeremiah 29:11–13. What comes of surrendering to God's will and being obedient to Him?*

These passages reflect a life filled with God's peace, love, and joy. By committing your life to God, you can have the confidence that He will lead you in every decision and through even the most difficult circumstances. His path becomes your path (Proverbs 3:5,6).

When you are submitted to the Lord's will for your life, you are filled with the joy of knowing that God's plans for you are for plenty, hope, and a real future (Jeremiah 29:11). You can experience the "fellowship" of knowing that the Lord hears and answers your prayers. But this only happens when you get serious about committing every area of your life to Him and seeking Him with all your heart (verse 13).

8–8.   *Take a moment to memorize one of the above passages. Why did you select it and what does it mean to you?*

Read Romans 12:1,2. You can be a "living sacrifice" by trusting God completely and submitting the attitudes and actions of each day to Him. This does not have to be a drudgery at all, but a "spiritual act of worship." As you give yourself to God, He is able to transform your mind—and subsequent actions—and enable you to live for Him.

8–9.   *How is sacrificing your desires to God worship?*

Second Corinthians 5:15 sums up the message of this study: because Jesus Christ died for you, you owe Him your complete allegiance. This is your God-ordained purpose. And when you fulfill it, you will discover the joy of surrender.

Chapter Review

It is said that three powerful computers in Vatican City—Rafael, Michael, and Gabriel—host the web site of the Roman Catholic Church. These computers hold volumes of history, theology, liturgy, and press releases. But no matter how powerful or how packed with information they are, they cannot know or choose God's will. They were created to be technological servants of religion, not living participants in a decision to serve God.

You, however, are not a machine. You can accept or reject God's will. God created you with a free will. He never forces you to choose His plan, but He longs for you to accept His purposes and surrender to them.

Why does God want you to surrender to His will for you? Because He loves you. He expects the best from you and longs to make your life the best it can be. This can happen only when you surrender to Him and walk in His ways.

8–10. In the past, how have you done at surrendering to unpleasant aspects of God's will? How has this chapter encouraged you to submit your will to His regardless of what He asks?

Finding God's Will

A farmer was working in his field, looked up in the sky, and saw the clouds forming a giant letter *P* above him. He had been praying for God's will and took this as a sign that God wanted him to *p*reach. After several terribly frustrating, embarrassing preaching efforts, the farmer returned home discouraged. His pastor came by and suggested, "Perhaps that sign was from God. But maybe the giant *P* meant *p*lant and *p*low instead of *p*reach."

This is a whimsical story, but it makes a very serious point. You must carefully and prayerfully weigh every experience, sign, or supposed confirmation you think might indicate God's will. This chapter looks at the clear, knowable ways by which God reveals His will to believers.

Obeying God's Word

God's Word, the Bible, is God's revelation of himself to you. It contains many specific instructions, as well as many general principles, that will help you know and understand His will.

Read Psalm 119:1–8. If you keep "his statutes," God's Word can bring you happiness and contentment, helping you to be "blameless" (verses 1,2). Scripture demands your serious attention and obedience (verses 3,4). It is able to keep you from shame and in the very presence of God (verses 6,8).

9–1. *On what authority does the Bible deserve obedience? What does this indicate about its potential helpfulness in discovering God's will?*

With all these benefits from obeying God's Word, it is no wonder the Psalmist praised the Lord for it (verse 7). When you see how following Scripture can bring you blessing, you will be just as quick to thank God for it.

9–2. *Write a brief prayer of thanks for the guidance God can give through the Bible.*

9–3. *Read Psalm 119:101–105,133. What do these verses tell you about the intensity of love the Psalmist felt for God's Word? Do you have this kind of love for the Bible?*

Unless you spend time regularly and prayerfully reading God's Word, you cannot presume to think God will guide you through it on demand. You cannot use the Bible as some unsaved people use tarot cards, consulting it only when you want to make a decision. The Word must be "sweet" to you (verse 103).

God's Word is His personal revelation to the world about himself, His plan for humanity, and His plan for individual believers. As you spend time regularly reading Scripture and asking God to guide you, you can begin to experience the Bible as the "light for [your] path" (verse 105). As this becomes a reality, you will not only find God's purpose for you; you will also experience more power over temptation and freedom from problems with sin (verse 133).

9–4. *How can successfully resisting temptation by obeying God's Word help you to live in God's will?*

Relying On The Spirit's Direction

In addition to the Word of God, you have the presence of the Holy Spirit to guide you in finding and doing God's will. This was the promise that Jesus gave His disciples on the night He was arrested.

9–5.   *Read John 14:15–17. What do these verses tell you about the Holy Spirit? How is the presence of the Holy Spirit linked to your knowing and doing God's will?*

9–6.   *What do you think the title "Counselor" (verse 16) means in reference to the Holy Spirit in your life?*

The word translated "Counselor" in verse 16 can also be translated "Helper." It was a legal term used of anyone who helped another in trouble with the law. "Advisor" would be a way of thinking about this ministry of God's Spirit. You can rely on His help as you seek to know and do God's will.

In John 16:13,14, Jesus promised His followers that the Holy Spirit—whom He called the "Spirit of truth"—would reveal to them the things of God. The Spirit can explain these things to you, bringing glory to Christ as He does so.

In Acts 16:6–10, you can read how specific the Holy Spirit's guidance can be. Repeatedly, the Spirit prevented Paul and his ministry team from going to certain places and led them to others. Unlike the farmer's vision of a letter *P* in the clouds, the vision of the Macedonian man was clear and accurate (verses 9,10). The Holy Spirit may use visions or dreams to guide you, but He will most often lead you less obviously, as He led Paul to Troas and Europe by keeping him from entering Asia or Bithynia.

9–7. *Have you ever had a guiding dream or vision you thought God gave you? How did you find out whether or not it was truly from God?*

Seeking Godly Counsel

What could have helped the farmer interpret the cloud-formed *P* properly? If he had gone to his pastor first, he could have gotten wise advice from another believer's point of view. The godly counsel of mature believers is a safeguard for you, keeping you from rushing into what you might mistake for God's will.

9–8.   *Write about a time godly counsel either kept you from doing something foolish in the name of God or came after you did the foolish thing and taught you the value of getting advice from people who are also striving to obey.*

God never guides His people in a vacuum. Although He may have something very special in His plan for you, He has most likely done similar work in the lives of others—both in your lifetime and throughout the history of the Church. For this reason, you need to consult others when you are trying to determine God's will.

However, Proverbs 2:9–15 warns you to be cautious when you are given advice. Many people, ranging from those who are simply ignorant to those who are evil scam artists, parade under the guise of spirituality and deceptively lead believers astray (verses 12–15). Using wisdom will "protect you" (verse 11) from this kind of advice and show you what good advice is (verses 9,10).

9–9.   *Read Proverbs 22:17–21. What do these verses say about godly advisors and their role in helping you find God's will?*

Mentoring is a strong tradition reaching back through the history of the Church. A believer forms a relationship of trust with a more mature believer as his mentor. Because of the stability and godliness of his life, a mentor can be trusted to help you determine what God's will is for you.

This is not to say you become enslaved to one person's interpretation of God's will. A mentor must not be a dictator, but a reservoir of experience and wisdom. Most importantly, a spiritual mentor must point you to trust "in the Lord" (verse 19) and help you serve your Savior better (verse 21). Godly counsel must never be just another person's opinion, but the wise advice of a believer who is knowledgeable about God's Word and in tune with the Holy Spirit.

9–10. *List some mature Christians you know of your gender who meet the qualifications of a spiritual mentor. How could you develop close relationships with them?*

Chapter Review

Reexamine the ways you can find God's revealed will for you—studying the Bible, praying for the Spirit's guidance, observing your circumstances, and seeking the advice of mature Christians. Beyond the basic commands of God's Word, you will need to use all of these methods together to determine God's will for you.

*9–11. Make a "Top 10" list of goals for your life by category—
spiritual growth, career, ministry, relationships, etc.*

-

-

-

-

-

-

-

-

-

-

Once you have made your list, pray daily to determine which of these goals are part of God's will for you. Discuss the list with several other believers. Read the Bible to see what it has to say about the goals you wrote down (possibly using the topical study method).

Near the end of this week, cross out the goals that are yours alone and start concentrating your efforts on achieving the goals God has for you.

Part Four

Living By The Spirit

People often think of God as far removed, answering a prayer only when it strikes His fancy, but otherwise having little to do with the daily lives of humans, including those who believe in Him. But the Bible teaches a wonderful truth, one which brings God incredibly near. His Spirit is alive in the heart of all believers, desiring to work through them from the inside out!

What does this mean for you? It means you are not alone shouting up at a distant God. You do not face struggles and times of testing with your strength. You have not been left behind to argue people into accepting the gospel. Why? Because the Holy Spirit can fill and work through you.

As you will read in the final three chapters of this book, allowing the Spirit to fill and overflow you does take effort. But it is not effort you are forced to make unaided. You have been invited to cooperate with the immeasurably powerful Holy Spirit in living wholeheartedly for the Lord!

God wants all believers to be filled with His Holy Spirit.

Being Filled With The Spirit

Do you know what happens to a 5-gallon can when all of the air is pumped out of it? The space inside becomes a vacuum. Atmospheric pressure on the outside exerts 14.69 pounds of pressure per square inch on the can. Without an equal amount of pressure within, the can is crushed as though squeezed by a giant, invisible hand.

Life itself is full of pressures. Building a career, paying off your education, developing your marriage, raising a family, and paying bills are just some of the normal pressures of an adult. When problems come—illness, accidents, job losses, family breakups—the pressure can be almost unbearable.

10–1. What are some of the crushing pressures you have faced recently?

What is the answer? How can you deal with the pressures of life without caving in? When the squeeze is on, you need more than theory to face the realities of life.

God's answer is to fill you with a force greater than the destructive forces around you. When you have the Holy Spirit in you, the pressure is equalized—and then some. You are not only equal to the challenges through His divine power, you are more than a conqueror! God can enable you to do more than simply hold your own. In His name, you can make a difference in your world.

Christ And The Holy Spirit

Jesus understood the spiritual hunger of the people in His day. Religious ritual was not enough to satisfy their inner longings to know God. Their legalism did not release divine blessing: it stifled it. Faithful Jews looked to the temple and to their religious leaders for help, but it was not there. The people desired a deeper relationship with God.

10–2. Does this description seem appropriate for your Christian walk lately? How do you feel about that?

In John 7:37–39, Jesus identified himself as the source of true spiritual fulfillment. "If anyone is thirsty, let him come to me and drink" (verse 37). Jesus refreshes those who will come to Him. When you drink of His Holy Spirit, you fill your own spiritual reservoir and become a source of life-giving water for others.

10–3. Describe a Christian you know and admire who exemplifies this kind of joy- and Spirit-filled life.

Jesus knew His followers would face intense persecution for His sake. They would need help if they were to remain steadfast in their faith and fulfill their mission in the world.

Take a look at John 14:15–17 and John 16:7. Jesus had no intention of leaving the disciples to face the battle alone. He would send divine reinforcements. The Comforter would come—not only to be with them, but to dwell in them.

10–4. What has this promise meant to you when you have been discouraged?

In order to receive the Spirit's fullness, you must humbly recognize your need for divine strength and be willing to seek Him. You must tap the flow of supernatural enabling.

Without Him, you cannot endure the pressures of life. In His power, you can stand; without Him, you crumble.

The Spirit And Early Christians

Did Jesus keep His promise to send the Comforter? According to Acts 2:1–4, He certainly did.

The Holy Spirit came on the Day of Pentecost. The sound of a mighty wind and the appearance of flames of fire over each of the believers marked His coming. However, these signs, reminiscent of Old Testament manifestations of God's presence, were not to become standard evidence of the Spirit's outpouring. A more personal sign, speaking with other tongues, would become the indicator of the Spirit's infilling.

10–5. In light of the chapter on surrendering to God, why do you think God chose speaking in tongues as evidence that a believer has been baptized in the Spirit?

Although the disciples did not understand what they were saying, foreign-born Jews in Jerusalem did. They were amazed that Galileans were speaking their languages, and they questioned the meaning of this strange occurrence.

Some people ridiculed. Newly filled with the Holy Spirit, Peter stood before those gathered in Jerusalem that day for the Feast of Harvest and proclaimed the message of Christ to them. His fear was gone. The believers were no longer intimidated by Jewish authorities. The Holy Spirit had put them on the offensive. The power within was greater than the dangers around them. Peter led 3,000 people to the Lord. Many sealed their commitment with the witness of water baptism.

10–6. What does this say about one of the major reasons God wants to fill you with His Spirit?

The Day of Pentecost was only the beginning. The Holy Spirit remained with the disciples, enabling them to speak boldly for God and punctuating their testimonies with the miraculous. As Jesus prophesied in Acts 1:8, the message spread to Samaria. These people, who had long been despised by the Jews, also received the gift of the Holy Spirit (8:14–17).

Perhaps the greatest surprise of all was the revelation that God's gift of the Spirit was also intended for the Gentiles. At first Peter resisted the idea. Then he realized God is no respecter of persons. As he preached at the home of the Roman centurion Cornelius, the Holy Spirit interrupted the meeting. The Jewish believers knew God was at work. They heard the Gentiles "speaking in tongues and praising God" just as they had done (10:46).

The same scene was repeated in Ephesus when Paul met with believers there (see 19:1–7). The Ephesians had never heard of the Holy Spirit. But when Paul laid his hands on them and encouraged them to receive God's gift, the Holy Spirit gave them the ability to glorify God in a new language.

10–7. Of the instances of believers being baptized in the Spirit recorded in Acts, which one means the most to you? Why?

The Holy Spirit And You

Like Peter's audience on the Day of Pentecost, you may have the desire to receive the gift of the Holy Spirit. But what are the prerequisites for being filled with the Spirit?

Peter's first instruction to his listeners was: "Repent!" To repent means to change your mind and attitudes toward sin and righteousness. In order to have God's fullness, you must turn from sinful pursuits. God's gift is for those who love and obey Him.

10–8. What are some things you know you need to repent of before God in order to open yourself to the Spirit?

Peter then told the new believers to be baptized in water. Though water baptism is not a requirement for salvation or for the baptism in the Holy Spirit, it is important as a public witness of your determination to follow Jesus Christ.

Having changed their position from unbelief to faith, the converts were ready to receive the gift of the Holy Spirit. No other ceremony was necessary. No waiting period was required.

God looks on the heart. When you have placed your total confidence in Him and have turned from every wrong action and attitude, you have only to reach out and receive the Holy Spirit. God's promise is for all who have responded to the divine call to follow Jesus (Acts 2:37–39).

10–9. Does this mean you need to be perfect before you can be filled with the Holy Spirit? Explain your reasoning.

The human heart hungers for satisfaction and joy. Those who do not know Christ look for happiness in all the wrong places. The search for joy often leads to deeper despair and even to suicide. So where can satisfaction and joy be found? God desires to give His joy to those who will receive it. The apostle Paul knew the source of lasting joy, and he stated it in Ephesians 5:18: "Do not get drunk on wine, which leads to debauchery. Instead, be filled with the Spirit."

The side effects of alcohol and drug use are well known. Any pleasure found in these chemicals carries a high price tag. Being filled with the Holy Spirit, however, brings only blessing and benefit. It produces singing, thanksgiving, and wholesome attitudes that promote harmony and healing in personal relationships.

Chapter Review

Life is full of problems. When you have a spiritual void in your life, those problems can crush you. But when you are filled with the Holy Spirit, you can withstand those problems. You can serve God boldly. You can proclaim Him to your friends without fear.

God has made the promise of the Holy Spirit available to everyone, including you. The only requirement is that you have given your life to Him. You must believe in the Lord, trust Him for salvation, and walk in obedience to His will.

God wants you to be filled with His Spirit. The full joy of constantly living in His presence can be yours. The inner strength to face life's challenges can be yours. God is more than willing to give this supernatural empowerment. Are you ready to receive it?

10–10. *If you have not been baptized in the Holy Spirit, get other believers to join in asking the Lord to fill you completely. Use the space below to record what happens and when it occurs.*

The Holy Spirit uses a variety of means to guide believers.

Following The Spirit's Lead

A tourist set out on his own to see the sites of a great city. After a few hours of walking through the shops and taking photographs of various ancient sites, he realized he could not find his way back to his hotel. He tried asking several people for directions, but was frustrated at his unfamiliarity with the language. All their efforts to help proved futile.

Finally, the tourist found a taxi driver able to take him back to his hotel. That night while he massaged his aching feet, the weary tourist determined to secure an local guide before venturing into the city again.

The Holy Spirit is an invaluable Guide. He can provide you with spiritual wisdom, an understanding of Scripture, and direction for Christian service.

Giving You Spiritual Wisdom

In 1 Corinthians 2:9,10, the apostle Paul stated that what God has prepared for those who love Him is beyond normal human comprehension—a divine mystery. But His Spirit can let you in on God's secrets.

11-1. How has the Holy Spirit opened your understanding of spiritual things?

Some of the Corinthian believers were caught up in the so-called "deep wisdom" of the Greek philosophers. But only the Spirit has the ability to search out the deep things of God. He is also the only one who can give you insight into what God has planned for you (verse 11).

God also wants you to understand the blessings and gifts He has abundantly provided. Your spirit cannot understand these truths. But God has given you the Holy Spirit to help you understand what He has generously given to you (verse 12).

For Paul, spiritual truths cannot be communicated using human wisdom. To teach these truths, the apostle used words that were spiritual in nature (verse 13). Not only did the Holy Spirit reveal spiritual truths to Paul, He also gave him the ability to proclaim these truths. God's message depends totally on the Spirit for understanding and proclamation.

11-2. Has the Holy Spirit ever taken something you heard or read and made it come alive to you? What did this feel like?

You would have never experienced that illumination if you had not been a Christian. Unbelievers naturally think the things of the Spirit are foolishness (verse 14). They cannot understand spiritual truth because they do not have the Holy Spirit to reveal the things of God to them. But the spiritual person discerns the wisdom of God through the Holy Spirit. And, according to Paul, the world cannot judge you because they cannot properly discern spiritual things (verse 15).

11–3. *Think back to before you were a Christian. How well did you understand basic Christian concepts? How is it different for you now that you are a believer?*

Those who consider themselves wise in this world often place themselves in a position of authority in judging the purpose and place of the Church in society. But because they do not understand God's wisdom and knowledge, they do not have sound judgment. In verse 16, Paul compared the world attempting to instruct the Church with the foolishness of humans attempting to instruct God.

As a believer, you can know the mind of God. Some have misused this verse to promote their spiritual superiority. They claim they have the mind of God and insinuate that other believers do not. Knowing the mind of God simply means that you can understand His view of the Church and the world. And every believer can have this understanding through God's Spirit.

Revealing God's Word To You

During Jesus' 3 years with His disciples, He taught them many things about the kingdom of God. After His ascension, Jesus would send the Holy Spirit to help His disciples remember His teachings (John 14:25,26). In fact, the Holy Spirit would be their Teacher.

11–4. How do you feel the Holy Spirit has acted as a Teacher in your life? What kind of Teacher is the Holy Spirit?

Jesus had not told His disciples everything. In fact, He had many things that He still wanted to tell them, but they were not ready for this teaching (16:12). Perhaps they would have been overwhelmed if they understood everything that was yet to come. Possibly, though, there were some things they would only understand after Christ's resurrection.

11–5. Describe a time God told you something that you would not have been prepared to understand or accept earlier.

The disciples would have a Teacher: the Holy Spirit would teach them the things they needed to know. They could trust Him because He would only teach them what was true. The disciples could be assured of this because the Spirit would only speak the things which He heard.

11–6. *How does it make you feel to know the Holy Spirit will only teach you what is true?*

The Holy Spirit would also show these disciples things to come. This revelation gave these disciples insight into God's plan for the Church.

The Holy Spirit will not speak on His own, for He has come to glorify Christ (verse 14). The words that the Holy Spirit speaks come from Christ and God (verse 15). It is this truth that He proclaims to those who follow Christ.

The Holy Spirit can also lead you into all truth. He can give you an understanding of the Bible. You can learn from Him, and He can help you discern that which is not true. As you read God's Word, the Spirit can give you the guidance you need.

Directing You In Ministry

Many in the world today seek direction from horoscopes or psychics. As a follower of God, you can rely on direction from the Holy Spirit.

11–7. *In your opinion, how can you know you are being directed by the Holy Spirit?*

The Book of Acts is filled with accounts of the Holy Spirit guiding the lives of believers. Acts 8 records the great revival in Samaria. In verse 26, an angel instructed Philip to leave Samaria and head toward Gaza. Between Jerusalem and Gaza, Philip met an Ethiopian eunuch. In verse 29, the Spirit directed Philip to go to this Ethiopian's chariot. The result of this encounter was the salvation of this Ethiopian. This was no mere chance encounter; the Spirit clearly directed Philip. God had a special plan for Philip, who obeyed God's Spirit.

In Acts 10:19,20, the Holy Spirit instructed Peter to go with the three Gentile visitors to Cornelius' house. When Peter arrived, he discovered that Cornelius had gathered his relatives to hear the gospel. And while Peter preached the gospel, Cornelius and his family members were saved and filled with the Holy Spirit.

11–8. *Write a brief prayer dedicating yourself this week to being sensitive to nudges by the Spirit to witness.*

The Holy Spirit also directed local congregations. As the church at Antioch fasted and prayed, the Spirit instructed them to send Barnabas and Saul for a work to which God had called them (13:2–4). Luke does not tell exactly how the Spirit spoke in this situation. It could have been through one of the manifestation gifts of the Spirit or it could have been through an inner feeling that this was what the Spirit wanted them to do.

Another instance of the Spirit's direction is found in Acts 15. The Church was divided over the requirements for the Gentiles who were being saved. The apostles, elders, and members of the church in Jerusalem met in order to reach an agreement concerning this issue. The Judaizers believed the Gentiles should obey the law of Moses, especially in regard to circumcision, before they could be saved. Peter, Paul, and Barnabas, on the other hand, recognized the grace of God through faith. God spoke through these three men and the council concluded that salvation for the Gentiles came by faith alone. This decision was not made by human reasoning: the Holy Spirit directed this decision (verse 28).

11–9. *How can you as an individual believer contribute practically to your church's being guided by the Spirit?*

The Spirit can direct and guide your life if you will listen to His voice and follow His direction. What is recorded in Acts is there to show you that God is able to work among His people, and to encourage you to seek His will in your life today.

Chapter Review

The Holy Spirit knows what is best for you. Ask Him to direct your life according to God's plan for you. After you have made this request, listen for His voice. He may direct you through the Word or He may give you an inner peace or nudge to let you know that He is directing you.

11–10. After you have spent some time with the Lord this week, write below what you feel the Holy Spirit is guiding you to do.

When many are turning to worldly, even satanic, means for direction, remember God has given you His Holy Spirit to help you in your walk with Him. You can be assured that He will always lead you in the way of truth. He will never tell you to do anything contrary to God's Word.

Bearing Spiritual Fruit

What do you get when you mix peas with an Austrian monk? The first work in genetics. In the 1860s, Gregory Mendel observed a number of generations of pea plants and examined how traits were passed from "parent" to "child" plants. From this study, Mendel came up with the idea that there are naturally dominant and recessive genes. Dominant genes are those that show up in the next generation; recessive genes are hidden (at least for that generation).

Since the Fall, the dominant spiritual gene, so to speak, has been the desire to sin and has produced character traits that are ungodly. But now that you are a Christian, you need to make sin recessive and let the Holy Spirit be the dominant force in determining your character traits.

Galatians 5:16–21 provides a necessary background for the rest of this chapter. In this passage, you are exhorted to let your lifestyle as a Christian be dominated by the Holy Spirit instead of by your fallen human nature. Your freedom in Christ is not a freedom to indulge in sin, but to walk in the new life you enjoy through faith in Jesus Christ by His Spirit (see 1 Peter 2:16).

Being Loving

12–1. Read 1 Corinthians 13:1–8. How does the kind of love you show others compare to this love?

You can love like that, but not without help. The new life brought about in you by the Spirit is to be characterized by love. Love is the opposite of everything selfish; it motivates you to genuinely care about the unlovely, the provoking, and the unpromising as well as the lovable. It chooses the path of sacrifice and service. Patterned after Christ's own love for you, this fruit of the Spirit never seeks anything but the best even for those who seek the worst for you.

Being Joyful

12–2. How would you define the difference between happiness and joy? Which do you most often demonstrate?

Happiness is not permanent and is completely dependent on external circumstances. Joy, however, comes from within; it is of the Spirit. A Christian's joy is suggestive of spiritual gladness and delight because of one's relationship to God. It has nothing to do with your situation and everything to do with your satisfaction in the Lord.

Being At Peace

This wonderful fruit is a deep sense of spiritual well-being, an awareness that you are in right relationship with God. Peace is an unshakable tranquillity of heart and mind which stems from the consciousness that every aspect of your life is in the hands of a benevolent God.

The story is told of a first century martyr who, as the fire was being lit around him, asked the officer in charge to place his hand over his heart. Its steady, quiet beat so amazed the executioner that he, too, later became a Christian.

12–3. How have you developed more peace as you have grown as a Christian?

Being Patient

Here is God's answer to emotional "burn out." The Holy Spirit can enable you to bear the unceasing stresses and strains of life. In the fruit of patience, you can discover a God-given ability to triumphantly endure insult and injustice at the hands of others. (All of this is available without your having to losing your joy!) Patience is a Spirit-manufactured endurance. It is the ability to hold on, to put up with the weaknesses encountered in others and the irritations that otherwise cause tempers to flare and angry words to flow.

12–4. Write about a difficult or frustrating situation you have experienced and how the Spirit helped you with patience.

Being Kind

12–5. How would you rate yourself in genuine kindness?

Kindness is generosity of spirit, being courteous to and considerate of others. It demonstrates itself in a quiet wisdom that draws people together and closer to God. It is also the disposition of love that reaches out a strong but gentle hand to those struggling with sin.

Watch Jesus in His dealings with Nathaniel, Nicodemus, the woman at the well, and Zacchaeus. The Holy Spirit will equip you also for showing kindness in all you do and toward all the people you meet.

Being Good

Some Christians think they must withdraw from contact with worldly people if they are to keep themselves pure. Jesus, however, lived in constant contact with people of all sorts. In fact, one of the miracles of His life was that He lived it without compromise and without sin.

12–6. How has the Holy Spirit helped you overcome past temptations to do wrong instead of doing what is good?

The fruit of goodness is a Spirit-enabled ability to live out your life in a wicked world while producing a rich harvest of righteous deeds. Such deeds present convincing proof to the unbeliever of the reality of what Jesus has done in you.

Being Faithful

Being assured of God's absolute trustworthiness inevitably leads to faithfulness in your own life after the pattern of

God's character. The fruit of faithfulness identifies itself as constancy, trustworthiness, dependability, and reliability. Faithfulness is loyalty to both God and your peers that does not waver in its commitment.

12–7. Who are five people with whom you need to increase your faithfulness? Ask the Holy Spirit to help you do this.

Being Gentle

In classical Greek, the word for gentleness (or meekness) was used of a powerful animal that had been tamed, trained, and brought under control. This is an excellent illustration of the word used by Paul in Galatians. This fruit of the Spirit speaks of a mastery of the human spirit which Christ alone can do. It shows a strength of character, clothed with true humility, which seeks the good of others as it would its own.

12–8. Describe your own metaphor for gentleness as defined in the above paragraph.

Being Self-Controlled

The life submitted to the direction of the Spirit strives to keep its own desires in proper perspective. The spiritual fruit of self-control enables you to have mastery over natural appetites, impulses, and desires rather than allowing these things to master you. It permits the Holy Spirit to moderate your life so that you will not be guilty of sins of personal excess. It often requires self-discipline in matters of daily habit so that God will be honored in your holy living.

12–9. In what areas have you been undisciplined? How can you make practical improvements—with the help of the Holy Spirit—in one of these areas this week?

Chapter Review

Two ideas must be kept in balance as you think of the fruit of the Spirit. First, it is of the Spirit. It is not something that is self-generated. God does not ask you to live the Christian life until you have received the gift of new life which He offers you through Christ.

Fruitfulness will flow naturally from the Spirit's living within you. You may be able to manufacture fake fruit, but only God can bring the real thing into being through the power of the Holy Spirit.

Second, the Holy Spirit can only produce His fruit in your life as much as you cooperate with and submit to His control in your life. An element of mystery shrouds an orchard laden with fruit or a flower garden with its galaxy of colors and fragrances. But the abundance of fruit is never an accident. Careful and time-consuming cultivation has to take place first in order for fruit to flourish. No short cuts to spiritual fruitfulness are available either. It requires daily submission on your part to ensure that the Spirit has freedom to produce His harvest.

12-10. Which of the fruit of the Holy Spirit have you been trying to produce lately on your own? Surrender them to the Lord, pledging to allow the Spirit to bring them forth in your life.

Notes

Notes